READING AND WRITING MUSIC

50 Ready-to-Use Activities
for Grades 3–9

READING AND WRITING MUSIC

50 Ready-to-Use Activities for Grades 3–9

Audrey J. Adair

Illustrated by Leah Solsrud

MUSIC CURRICULUM ACTIVITIES LIBRARY

PARKER PUBLISHING COMPANY
West Nyack, New York 10994

Library of Congress Cataloging-in-Publication Data

Adair, Audrey J.
    Reading and writing music.
    ISBN 0-13-762196-5
    (Music curriculum activities library ; unit 2)
    1. School music—Instruction and study.   2. Musical
notation.   3. Sight-reading (Music) I. Title. II. Series:
Adair, Audrey J.,   Music curriculum
activities library ; unit 2.
    MT10.A14   1987   unit 2   87-8830
    372.8′7 s [372.8′7]   CIP

Printed in the United States of America

10   9   8   7   6

ISBN 0-13-762196-5

PARKER PUBLISHING COMPANY
West Nyack, NY 10994

A Simon & Schuster Company

On the World Wide Web at http://www.phdirect.com

Prentice-Hall International (UK) Limited, *London*
Prentice-Hall of Australia Pty. Limited, *Sydney*
Prentice-Hall Canada Inc., *Toronto*
Prentice-Hall Hispanoamericana, S.A., *Mexico*
Prentice-Hall of India Private Limited, *New Delhi*
Prentice-Hall of Japan, Inc., *Tokyo*
Simon & Schuster Asia Pte. Ltd., *Singapore*
Editora Prentice-Hall do Brasil, Ltda., *Rio de Janeiro*

About the Author

Audrey J. Adair has taught music at all levels in the Houston, Texas, and Dade County, Florida, public schools. She has served as a music consultant, music specialist, general music instructor, choir director, and classroom teacher. In addition, she has written a series of musical programs for assemblies and holiday events, conducted music workshops, organized music programs for the community, established glee club organizations, and done specialization work with gifted and special needs students. Currently, she directs and coordinates children's choirs, performs as soloist with flute as well as voice, and composes sacred music.

Mrs. Adair received her B.A. in Music Education from St. Olaf College in Northfield, Minnesota, and has done graduate work at the University of Houston and Florida Atlantic University in Fort Lauderdale. She is also the author of *Ready-to-Use Music Activities Kit* (Parker Publishing Company), a resource containing over 200 reproducible worksheets to teach basic music skills and concepts.

About the *Library*

The *Music Curriculum Activities Library* was developed for you, the busy classroom teacher or music specialist, to provide a variety of interesting, well-rounded, step-by-step activities ready for use in your music classroom. The *Library*'s seven carefully planned Units combine imagination, motivation, and student involvement to make learning as exciting as going on a field trip and as easy as listening to music.

The units of the *Music Curriculum Activities Library* are designed to be used separately or in conjunction with each other. Each Unit contains 50 *all new* ready-to-use music activity sheets that can be reproduced as many times as needed for use by individual students. These 350 illustrated, easy-to-read activities will turn even your most reluctant students into eager learners. Each Unit offers a wealth of information on the following topics:

Unit 1: *Basic Music Theory* develops an understanding of the basic elements of melody, rhythm, harmony, and dynamics.

Unit 2: *Reading and Writing Music* provides a source of reinforcement and instills confidence in the beginner performer through a wide range of note-reading and writing activities in the treble clef, bass clef, and in the clef of one's own instrument.

Unit 3: *Types of Musical Form and Composition* gives the student the foundation needed to enjoy worthwhile music by becoming acquainted with a wide variety of styles and representative works.

Unit 4: *Musical Instruments and the Voice* provides knowledge of and insight into the characteristic sounds of band, orchestra, folk instruments, and the voice.

Unit 5: *Great Composers and Their Music* familiarizes the student with some of the foremost composers of the past and present and their music; and cultivates an early taste for good music.

Unit 6: *Special Days Throughout the Year* offers the student well-illustrated, music-related activities that stimulate interest and discussion about music through holidays and special occasions for the entire school year.

Unit 7: *Musicians in Action* helps the student examine music as a pastime or for a career by exploring daily encounters with music and the skills, duties, environment, and requirements of a variety of careers in music.

How to Use the *Library*

The activities in each Unit of the *Library* may be sequenced and developed in different ways. The general teacher may want to use one activity after the other, while the music specialist may prefer to use the activities in conjunction with the sequencing of the music curriculum. Teachers with special or individualized needs may select activities from various Units and use them over and over before actually introducing new material.

Let's take a closer look at how you can use the *Music Curriculum Activities Library* in your particular classroom situation:

... For THE MUSIC TEACHER who is accountable for teaching classes at many grade levels, there is a wide range of activities with varying degrees of difficulty. The activity sheets are ideal to strengthen and review skills and concepts suitable for the general music class.

... For THE NEW TEACHER STARTING A GENERAL MUSIC CLASS, these fun-filled activities will provide a well-balanced, concrete core program.

... For THE SPECIALIZED TEACHER who needs to set definite teaching goals, these activities offer a wealth of information about certain areas of music, such as career awareness, composers, and musical forms.

... For THE BAND AND CHOIR DIRECTOR, these activity sheets are a valuable resource to explore band, orchestra, and folk instruments, along with the singing voice.

... For THE PRIVATE MUSIC TEACHER who wants to sharpen and improve students' note reading skills, the *Library* offers ample homework assignments to give students the additional practice they need. There are many activity sheets using the clef of one's instrument and theory pages with illustrations of the keyboard.

... For THE MUSIC CONSULTANT using any one of the units, there are plenty of activities specifically correlated to the various areas of music providing reinforcement of learning. The activity sheets are suitable for class adoption in correlation with any music book series.

... For THE THEORY TEACHER, there are activities to show the students that music analysis is fun and easy.

... For THE TEACHER WHO NEEDS AN ADEQUATE MEANS OF EVALUATING STUDENT PROGRESS, there are fact-filled activities ideal for diagnostic purposes. A space is provided on each sheet for a score to be given.

. . . For THE CLASSROOM TEACHER with little or no musical background, the *Library* offers effective teaching with the flexibility of the seven units. All that has to be done is to decide on the music skill or concept to be taught and then duplicate the necessary number of copies. Even the answers can be duplicated for self-checking.

. . . For THE SUBSTITUTE TEACHER, these sheets are ideal for seatwork assignments because the directions are generally self-explanatory with minimal supervision required.

. . . For THE INSTRUCTOR OF GIFTED STUDENTS, the activities may be used for any type of independent, individualized instruction and learning centers. When used in an individualized fashion, the gifted student has an opportunity to pursue music learning at his or her own pace.

. . . For THE TEACHER OF SPECIAL EDUCATION, even the disadvantaged and remedial student can get in on the fun. Each concept or skill will be mastered as any lesson may be repeated or reinforced with another activity. Some of these activity sheets are designed to provide success for students who have difficulty in other subject areas.

. . . For the INDIVIDUAL who desires to broaden and expand his or her own knowledge and interest in music, each Unit provides 50 activities to help enjoy music.

The *Music Curriculum Activities Library* is ideally a teacher's program because a minimum of planning is required. A quick glance at the Contents in each Unit reveals the titles of all the activity sheets, the ability level necessary to use them, and the skills involved for each student. Little knowledge of music is generally needed to introduce the lessons, and extensive preparation is seldom necessary. You will, of course, want to read through the activity before presenting it to the class. In cases where you need to give information about the activity, two different approaches might be considered. (1) Use the activity as a basis for a guided discussion before completing the activity to achieve the desired results, or (2) Use the activity as a foundation for a lesson plan and then follow up by completing the activity. Either one of these approaches will enhance your own and your students' confidence and, by incorporating a listening or performing experience with this directed study, the students will have a well-rounded daily lesson.

All activity sheets throughout the *Library* have the same format. They are presented in an uncluttered, easy-to-read fashion, with self-explanatory directions. You need no extra materials or equipment, except for an occasional pair of scissors. The classroom or resource area should, however, contain a few reference books, such as song books or music series' books, encyclopedias, reference books about composers, a dictionary, music dictionary or glossary, and so on, so that while working on certain activities the student has easy access to resource books. Then, you simply need to duplicate the activity sheet as many times as needed and give a copy to each student. Even paper grading can be kept to a minimum by reproducing the answer key for self-checking.

The collection of activities includes practice in classifying, matching, listing, researching, naming, drawing, decoding, identifying, doing picture or crossword puzzles, anagrams, word searches, musical word squares, and much much more.

These materials may be used successfully with students in grades 3 and up. The activities and artwork are intentionally structured to appeal to a wide range of ages. For this reason, no grade-level references appear on the activity sheets so that you can use them in a variety of classroom settings, although suggested ability levels (beginner, intermediate, advanced) appear in the Contents.

The potential uses for the *Library* for any musical purpose (or even interdisciplinary study) are countless. Why? Because these activities allow you to instruct an entire class, a smaller group within the classroom, or individual students. While you are actively engaged in teaching one group of students, the activity sheets may be completed by another group. In any kind of classroom setting, even with the gifted music student or the remedial child, no student needs to sit idle. Now you will have more time for individual instruction.

The Units may be used in a comprehensive music skills program, in an enrichment program, or even in a remedial program. The *Library* is perfect for building a comprehensive musicianship program, improving basic music skills, teaching career awareness, building music vocabulary, exploring instruments, developing good taste in listening to music, appreciating different types of music, creating a positive learning environment, and providing growing confidence in the performer.

What Each Unit Offers You

A quick examination of the **Contents** will reveal a well balanced curriculum. Included are the titles of all activities, the level of difficulty, and the skill involved. The exception to this is Unit 6, where the date and special day, rather than the skill, are listed with the title of each activity.

Each of the **50 reproducible activity sheets** generally presents a single idea, with a consistent format and easy-to-follow directions on how to do the activity, along with a sufficient amount of material to enable the student to become proficient through independent and self-directed work. Because each activity has but one single behavioral objective, mastery of each skill builds confidence that allows the learner to continue progressively toward a more complete understanding of the structure of music, appreciation of music, and its uses. The activity sheets are just the right length, too, designed to be completed within a class period.

The **Progress Chart** provides a uniform, objective method of determining what skills have been mastered. With the aid of this chart, you will be able to keep track of goals, set priorities, organize daily and weekly lesson plans, and track assignments. The Progress Chart lists each activity and skill involved, and has a space for individual names or classes to be recorded and checked when each activity and skill is complete. The Progress Chart is ideal for accurate record keeping. It provides a quick, sure method for you to determine each individual student's achievements or weaknesses.

Use the **Teacher's Guide** for practical guidance on how the particular Unit will work for you. An easy effective learning system, this guide provides background information and reveals new techniques for teaching the Unit.

Throughout the *Library*, each **Answer Key** is designed with a well-thought-out system for checking students' answers. While some activities are self-checking without the use of the Answer Key, other activities can easily be student corrected, too, by simply duplicating the answer page and cutting apart the answers by activity number.

The Self-Improvement Chart provides the student with a self-assessment system that links curriculum goals with individual goals. By means of an appraisal checklist, the chart gives the student and teacher alike the key to finding individual talent. It also measures accountability. Included in the chart are (1) a method for recording goals and acquired music skills; (2) a log for attendance at special music events; (3) a music and instrument check-out record; (4) a log for extra credit activities and music projects; (5) a record of special music recognition awards, incentive badges, Music Share-a-Grams, Return-a-Grams; and (6) a record of music progress.

These specific features of the chart will help you:

- Provide a uniform, objective method of determining rewards for students.
- Assess future curriculum needs by organizing long-term information on student performance.
- Foster understanding of why students did or did not qualify for additional merit.
- Motivate students by giving them feedback on ways for self-improvement.
- Assist students in making statements of their own desires and intentions for learning, and in checking progress toward their goals.

The **Music Share-a-Gram** is a personalized progress report addressed to the parent and created to show the unique qualities of the individual child. It allows you to pinpoint areas of success and tell parents what they need to know about their child. The Music Share-a-Gram evaluates twelve important abilities and personal traits with ratings from exceptional to unsatisfactory, which you might want to discuss with students to solicit their reaction. For example, you might use these ratings as a basis for selecting a student to attend the gifted program in music. This form is designed to be sent with or without the Return-a-Gram, and may be hand-delivered by the student or sent through the mail. For easy record keeping, make a copy of the Gram and attach it to the back of the Student Record Profile Chart.

The **Return-a-Gram** is designed to accompany the Music Share-a-Gram and is sent to the parent on special occasions. When a reply is not expected or necessary, simply detach the Return-a-Gram before sending the Share-a-Gram. This form encourages feedback from the parent and even allows the parent to arrange for a parent-teacher conference. Both Grams are printed on the same page and are self-explanatory—complete with a dotted line for the parent to detach, fill in, and return.

The **Student Record Profile Chart** is a guide for understanding and helping students, and offers a means of periodic evaluation. The chart is easy to use and provides all you need for accurate record keeping and measuring accountability for individual student progress throughout all seven units. It provides an accumulative skills profile for the student and represents an actual score of his or her written performance for each activity. Here is a workable form that you can immediately tailor to your own requirements for interpretation and use of scores. Included are clear instructions, with an example, to help you record your students' assessment on a day-to-day basis, to keep track of pupil progress, and to check learning patterns over a period of time. This chart allows you to spot the potential superior achiever along with the remedial individual. The chart coordinates all aspects of data ranging from the students' name, class, school, classroom teacher's name, semester, date, page number, actual grade, and attendance.

The **Word List** is presented as a reinforcement for building a music vocabulary. It emphasizes the use of dictionary skills; the students make a glossary of important words related to the particular unit. Its purpose is to encourage the use of vocabulary skills by helping develop an understanding of the music terms, concepts, and names found on the activity sheets. This vocabulary reference page is meant to be reproduced and used by the individual student throughout the units as a guide for spelling, word recognition, pronunciation, recording definitions, plus any other valuable information. Throughout six units of the *Library*, a cumulation of the words are presented on the Word List pages. (A Word List is not included in Unit 6.) With the help of this extensive vocabulary, when the student uses the words on both the activity page and the Word List, they will become embedded as part of his or her language.

Each Unit contains a wide-ranging collection of **Incentive Badges**. Use them to reward excellence, commend effort, for bonuses, prizes, behavior modification, or as reminders. These badges are designed to capture the interest and attention of the entire school. Several badges are designed with an open-ended format to provide maximum flexibility in meeting any special music teaching requirement.

Included in each Unit is a simple **Craft Project** that may be created by the entire class or by individual students. Each craft project is an integral part of the subject matter of that particular unit and will add a rich dimension to the activities. The materials necessary for the construction of the craft projects have been limited to those readily available in most classrooms and call for no special technical or artistic skills.

PLUS each Unit contains:

- Worked-out sample problems for students to use as a standard and model for their own work.

- Additional teaching suggestions in the Answer Key for getting the most out of certain activities.

- Extra staff paper for unlimited use, such as composing, ear training, improvising, or writing chords.

- Activities arranged in a sequential pattern.

Resources for Teaching Music More Effectively

- Have a classroom dictionary available for reference.
- Have a glossary or music dictionary available for reference.
- Use only one activity sheet per class session.
- Distribute the Word List prior to the first activity sheet of the particular unit. Encourage students to underline familiar words on the list and write definitions or identifications on the back before instruction on the unit begins. Later, the students can compare their answers with those studied.
- Provide short-term goals for each class session and inform students in advance that awards will be given for the day. You'll see how their conduct improves, too.
- Encourage students to make or buy an inexpensive folder to store music activity sheets, craft projects, word lists, self-evaluation charts, and so on. Folders might be kept in the classroom when not in use and distributed at the beginning of each class period.
- Many of the activities are ideal for bulletin board display. If space is not available to display all students' work, rotate the exhibits.
- Encourage students to re-read creative writing pages for clarity and accuracy before copying the final form on the activity sheet. Proofreading for grammatical and spelling errors should be encouraged.
- For creative drawing activities, encourage students to sketch their initial ideas on another sheet of paper first, then draw the finished product on the activity sheet. It is not necessary to have any technical ability in drawing to experience the pleasure of these creative activities.
- Although you will probably want to work through parts of some activities with your students, and choose some activities for group projects, you will find that most lessons are designed to lead students to the correct answers with little or no teacher direction. Students can be directed occasionally to work through an activity with a partner to search out and correct specific errors.
- Self-corrections and self-checking make a much better impression on young learners than do red-penciled corrections by the classroom music teacher.
- On activities where answers will vary, encourage students to rate their own work on correctness, originality, completeness, carefulness, realism, and organization.

• Most activity pages will serve as a "teacher assistant" in developing specific skills or subject areas to study. The activities throughout the series are complete with learning objectives and are generally factual enough for the teacher to use as a basis for a daily lesson plan.

• The library research activities promote creativity instead of copying while students search out relevant data from a variety of sources, such as encyclopedias, dictionaries, reference books, autobiographies, and others. These activities are ideal for the individual student or groups of students working beyond the classroom environment.

• The following are practical guidelines in planning, organizing, and constructing the Craft Projects:

 . . . Acquaint yourself with any of the techniques that are new to you before you ask your students to undertake the project.

 . . . Decide on your project and assemble the materials before you begin.

 . . . Make a sample model for experience.

 . . . Use a flat surface for working.

 . . . Be sure the paper is cut exactly to measurements and that folds are straight.

 . . . Be available for consultation.

 . . . Provide guidance on what the next logical step is to encourage all students to finish their projects.

 . . . Use the finished craft projects as displays and points of interest for your school's open house.

• Many of the Incentive Badges found in each Unit are open-ended and can be made effective communication tools to meet your needs. Extra space is provided on these badges for additional written messages that might be used for any number of reasons. Be creative for your own special needs; load the copier with colored paper and print as many as you need for the semester or entire school year. Then simply use a paper cutter to separate the badges and sort them out alphabetically. Make an alphabetical index on file card dividers using these titles. Next, arrange them in an accessible file box or shoe box, depending on the size needed. Include a roll of tape to attach the badge to the recipient.

Teacher's Guide to Unit 2

Reading and Writing Music is designed to support the music skills program in the music curriculum by teaching children how to read notes so that they can develop good music reading skills. This unit, like the others in the *Library*, offers a diverse content with activities ranging from picture clues and word searches to crossword puzzles. The activities are aimed at improving such skills as writing notes on lines and spaces, transcribing in octaves, naming notes, drawing notes, rearranging notes, and transcribing from one clef to another.

Acquiring basic knowledge in note reading is a fundamental part of music education. In most classrooms you will find that the overwhelming majority of students are not musicians. As almost all students listen to music, however, it is advisable for you to build on listening experiences while introducing and reinforcing note reading skills. Music theory of this nature should always be an integral part of music listening and performing.

Unit 2 is divided into four parts, according to the type of clef used: treble clef, bass clef, both clefs, and the clef of one's own instrument. This gives you the necessary flexibility for making it possible to adapt the material to any teaching situation. Depending on the needs of the individual student, you can select as much material from each part as you desire or have time for. The classroom music teacher, for example, may find the activities in the first and fourth parts most valuable, while the string teacher may use all four parts. The fourth part of this unit is a versatile section, as you may choose the clef if the student does not play an instrument, or you may leave the choice to the student. An illustration and description of both the treble and bass clefs along with commonly used instruments for each clef can be found in "Clefs for Commonly Used Instruments and Voices," following the Answer Key.

As a special teaching aid, *Reading and Writing Music* also features a study guide to provide visual impact for building note reading confidence and enthusiasm. There are three Study Guide Strips to be cut apart for individual study. The three strips illustrate note placement on the Treble (G) staff, the Bass (F) staff, and the Grand staff with keyboard. The notes on each are named. This direct feedback approach is particularly well suited to young students who have not yet learned to read notes. These strips may be used by students while completing an activity, as a device for self-checking, or simply as a pocket study guide.

For the classroom music teacher who teaches music only once or twice a week, progress in note reading will be slow. For a student who has never had any music training, note reading is almost suggestive of a foreign language. Even for a student who has had music lessons, it takes practice to become proficient at it. The activity sheets in Unit 2 direct the student in a gradual, logical progression from beginning note reading experiences to the more advanced. Be patient and use activities to link each class session to the next so that this continuity will provide the student with the feeling of moving forward. Do not feel you have to use all the activity sheets in this unit. It is better to concentrate on the part that is applicable to the needs of the student and learn those notes well before going on to the next. Unit 2 promotes the student's interest in music in a way that will increase his or her understanding as well as give encouragement to take music lessons, as the mystery of note reading has been removed.

Many of the note reading activities use words composed from the Music Alphabet (A B C D E F G). Encourage students to sing or play musical phrases using the letters. They can learn to sing or play the notes for many words, including CABBAGE, BAGGAGE, DECADE, AGED, BED, BEG, and BAG. While trying this approach to reading notes, advise students to write lines above the notes where they want to indicate the octave. Refer to activity sheets 2-1 and 2-2 for examples of how lines distinguish notes "high C" and above. Students will soon discover that some combinations of notes have a "better" musical sound than others. By using different types of notes, the beginning notes of songs can be formed. The word GAGE, for example, spells the beginning notes for "Silent Night, Holy Night." By this kind of experimentation, a student can improve his or her ear.

Contents

Activity Number/Title		Skill Involved	Type of Note Used	Level of Difficulty
Using the Treble (G) Clef				
2-1	IT'S YOUR GUESS	Naming notes from low C to high E	Whole	Beginner
2-2	ALIEN TALK	Naming notes from low C to high E	Whole	Beginner
2-3	CAN YOU PICTURE THAT?	Using letter names of notes to write words	Whole	Beginner
2-4	MUSICAL G CLEF ANAGRAM #1	Writing words on a grid from notes to figure out puzzle theme	Whole	Beginner
2-5	MUSICAL G CLEF ANAGRAM #2	Writing word on a grid from notes to figure out puzzle theme	Whole	Beginner
2-6	MUSICAL G CLEF ANAGRAM #3	Writing words on a grid from notes to figure out puzzle theme	Whole	Beginner
2-7	NEW-AGE NAMES	Writing new names of the future using letter names of notes	Quarter	Beginner
2-8	MAKE A LIST	Creating a list of words from the Music Alphabet	Whole	Beginner
2-9	TREBLE CLEF PICTURE FUN	Writing names of objects using notes and note names	Whole	Beginner
2-10	NAME THE PERCUSSION	Writing names of percussion instruments using notes and note names	Quarter	Beginner
2-11	THE EEEEEASY CIRCLES	Unscrambling sets of notes to spell words	Quarter	Beginner

Contents

Activities for
USING THE TREBLE (G) CLEF

IT'S YOUR GUESS   2–1

Imagine you are baby sitting for a one-year-old. Use the note key to figure out the baby talk written in notation. Each group of notes spells a word. Write the answers on the blanks. Then, on the line below the blanks write what you think the one-year-old really meant to say.

NOTE KEY:

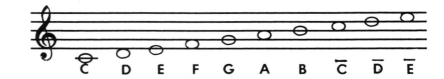

C D E F G A B C̄ D̄ Ē

BABY TALK:

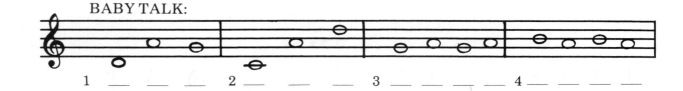

1 __ __ __   2 __ __ __   3 __ __ __ __   4 __ __ __ __

_____   _____   _____   _____

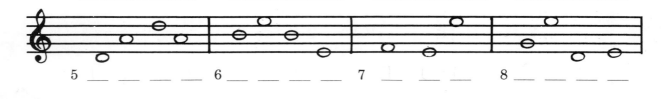

5 __ __ __ __   6 __ __ __   7 __ __ __   8 __ __ __

_____   _____   _____   _____

ALIEN TALK   2–2

Imagine you have just met a person from another planet. This alien sings different pitches as a way of talking to you. Use the note key below to decide what the alien is telling you. Write the letters to match the notes on the blanks below the staff. Each group of notes spells a word. On the back of this page write what you think the alien's message is.

NOTE KEY:

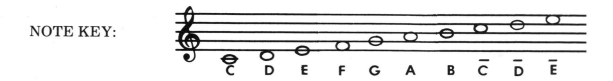

ALIEN'S WORDS:

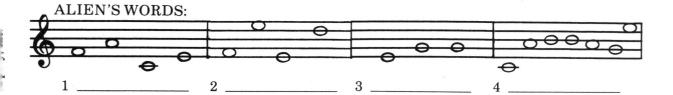

1 _____ 2 _____ 3 _____ 4 _____

5 _____ 6 _____ 7 _____ 8 _____

Draw a picture of a space ship and the alien.

CAN YOU PICTURE THAT?

Each group of numbers spells a word. Use the letter names of the notes on the staff to fill in the blanks of the missing words in the story.

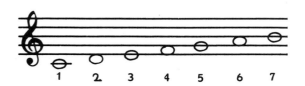

1   2   3   4   5   6   7

At ___ ___ ___ eight, ___ ___ ___ got a real birthday surprise from
   6 5 3   6 2 6

her ___ ___ ___. He planned a trip to the circus and arranged for her to go
   2 6 2

backstage to see ___ ___ ___ ___ the ___ ___ ___ lion. ___ ___ ___ loved lions. Her
      7 3 7 3   7 6 2   6 2 6

___ ___ ___ room walls were covered with drawings and pictures of lions.
7 3 2

She even had a collection of toy lions. Some were stuffed animals and
others were ceramic. One little lion was her pride and joy. It was made

of china and the size of an ___ ___ ___. On the day of her birthday, they took a ___ ___ ___ to the circus.
             3 5 5   1 6 7

___ ___ ___'s ___ ___ ___ ___ lit up when she saw their desti-
6 2 6   4 6 1 3

nation. The ringmaster greeted them and said,
"Happy Birthday, young lady, I understand you

have a date to see ___ ___ ___ ___, the big ___ ___ ___ lion.
         7 3 7 3   7 6 2

"___ ___ ___?" she asked. Soon they saw ___ ___ ___ ___ in
 7 6 2   7 3 7 3

his ___ ___ ___ ___ , sound asleep in his king size ___ ___ ___.
   1 6 5 3   7 3 2

(Draw ___ ___ ___ ___ .)
     7 3 7 3

MUSICAL G CLEF ANAGRAM #1   2–4

Write the letter names of the following notes. You will find that each group of notes spells a word. Then write the words on the grid, arranging them in such a way that the first vertical column reveals something about the picture.

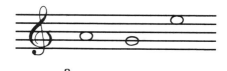

a. _____

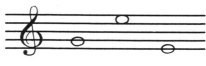

b. _____

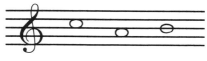

c. _____

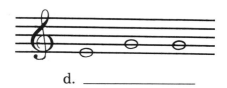

d. _____

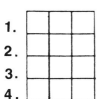

1.
2.
3.
4.

MUSICAL G CLEF ANAGRAM #2

Write the letter names of the following notes. You will find that each group of notes spells a word. Then write the words on the grid arranging them in such a way that the first vertical column reveals something about the picture.

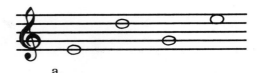

a. _____

b. _____

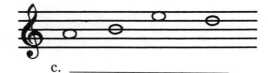

c. _____

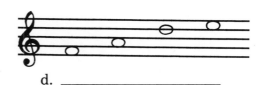

d. _____

1.
2.
3.
4.

Name _____

Date _____

MUSICAL G CLEF ANAGRAM #3

Write the letter names of the following notes. You will find that each group of notes spells a word. Then write the words on the grid arranging them in such a way that the first vertical column reveals something about the picture.

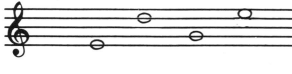

a. _____

b. _____

c. _____

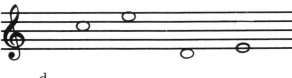

d. _____

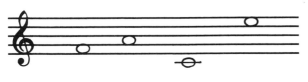

e. _____

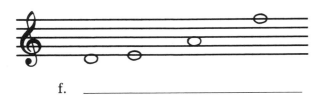

f. _____

1.			
2.			
3.			
4.			
5.			
6.			

The face of a building is called its _ _ _ _ _ _ .

Score _____

Class _____

Here are some new-age names written in notes for children born in the future. Write the names in the blanks. Then draw a picture of yourself in the window.

1. _____ 2. _____ 3. _____ 4. _____

5. _____ 6. _____ 7. _____ 8. _____

9. _____ 10. _____ 11. _____ 12. _____

Name _____

Date _____

Score _____

Class _____

MAKE A LIST

2–8

Write the letter names of the notes under the staff. Then, see how many words you can make from these letters. You may use the letters more than once in a word.

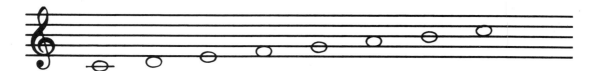

TREBLE CLEF PICTURE FUN   2-9

The names of these pictures can be spelled with notes. First print the name on the blank, using letters from the music alphabet. Allow spacing between the letters. Then from left to right, draw whole notes on the staff above their letter names.

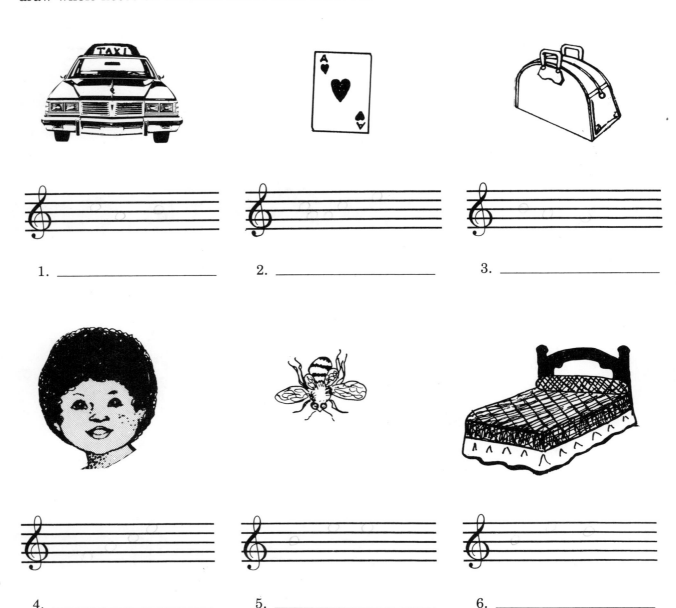

1. _____

2. _____

3. _____

4. _____

5. _____

6. _____

Name _____   Score _____

Date _____   Class _____

NAME THE PERCUSSION   2-10

The names of these percussion instruments have two or more letters missing. Finish writing the names using letters from the music alphabet. Then, above each of your letters, draw a matching quarter note. Watch the stem direction (♩♩).

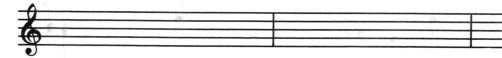

1. __ __ SS __ RUM   2. TRI __ N __ L __   3. __ YM __ __ LS

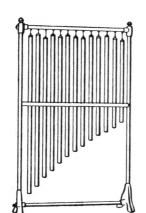 

4. __ HIM __ S   5. T __ M __ OURIN __   6. SN __ R __ __ RUM

THE EEEEEASY CIRCLES

The title of these puzzles gives you a clue in naming the circled blocks. Unscramble each set of notes on the staff to spell a four-letter word. Then write the words crosswise in the blocks on the grid.

A.   **B.**

1.
2.
3.
4.

1.    1.

2.    2.

3.    3.

4.    4.

WRITE THE ENDING

Write the ending to this story using at least five words with the music alphabet. Draw the staff and write the notes on it as in the example. Use the back of the page if you need extra space and give your story a title.

TITLE _____

Once there was a boy named
who would never eat his
Finally his mother said, "

ADD A LETTER

The letter names of each group of notes below spell a word with the first letter missing. That letter is from the music alphabet. Figure out what it is and draw the matching note on the staff. Then write the word on the line next to each staff.

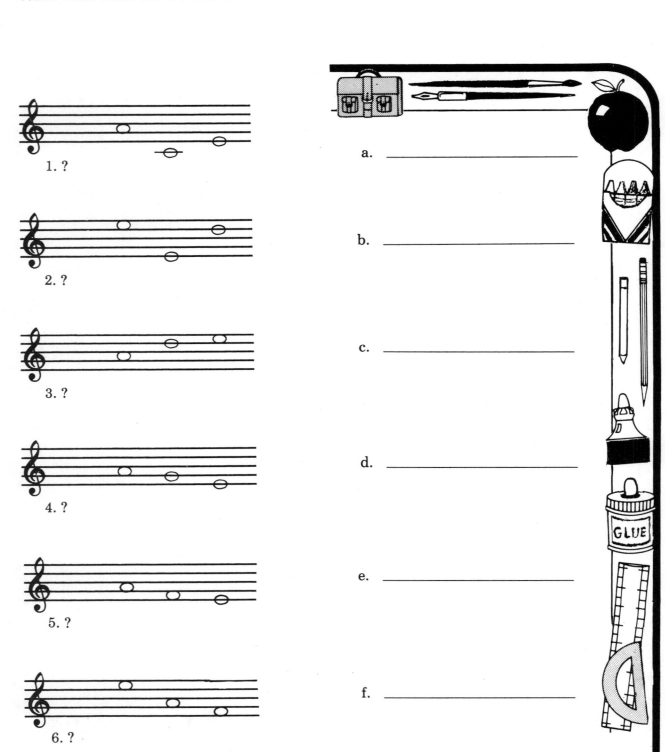

1. ?

2. ?

3. ?

4. ?

5. ?

6. ?

a. _____

b. _____

c. _____

d. _____

e. _____

f. _____

TREASURE HUNT

2–14

See how good you are in this treasure hunt. The letter names of each set of notes shown below spell a word, with the first letter missing. Write the letter names in the spaces under the notes. Then carefully select a letter from the treasure chest for the beginning sound of each word. Use each letter only once!

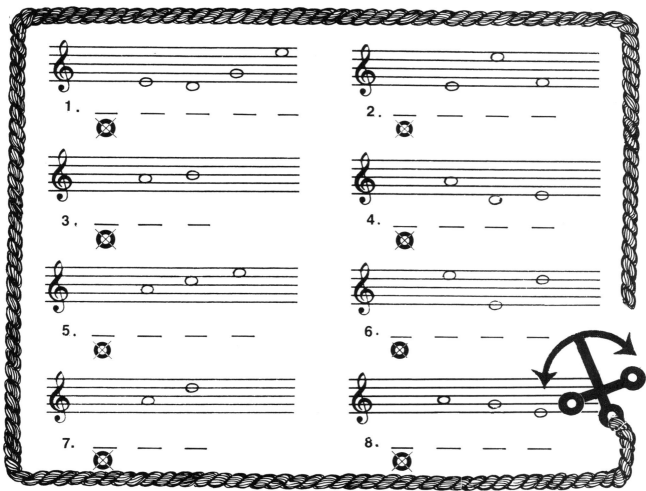

G CLEF PICTURE CLUE #1

Write the word under the staff that is suggested by the clue. All the letters in each word are from the music alphabet, except the last letter, which you place in the box. Then, draw matching whole notes on the staff above the letters in the blanks. The picture gives the clue for the word that will be spelled out in the boxes.

1. A small number; opposite of many.
2. In the past; gone by.
3. A wild animal known as a buck or doe.
4. Opposite of front.

1. ___ ___ ☐

2. ___ ___ ☐

3. ___ ___ ☐

4. ___ ___ ___ ☐

This painter is hard at ___ ___ ___ ___!

G CLEF PICTURE CLUE #2

Write the word under the staff that is suggested by the clue. All the letters are from the music alphabet except the first letter, which you place in the box. Then, draw matching whole notes on the staff above the letters in the blanks. The picture gives the clue for the word that will be spelled out in the boxes.

1. Free from harm or danger.
2. A useless plant.
3. Cooled with frozen water.
4. Built or formed.

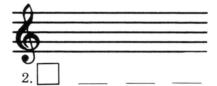

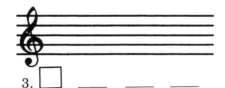

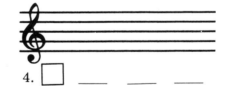

G CLEF PICTURE CLUE #3   2–17

Write the word under the staff that is suggested by the clue.
All letters are from the music alphabet except the first letter,
which you place in the box. Then, draw matching whole notes
on the staff above the letters in the blanks. The picture gives
the clue for the word that will be spelled out in the boxes.

1. The thickening of skin on the sole of a dog's foot.
2. A dignified poem that expresses a noble feeling.
3. Between the knee and the foot.
4. A young man.
5. Seaport in Honshu, Japan (rhymes with ruby).
6. A small flap.
7. Frozen water.
8. Strange or peculiar.
9. To snatch or grab suddenly.

1. ☐ ____ ____

2. ☐ ____ ____

3. ☐ ____ ____

4. ☐ ____ ____

5. ☐ ____ ____

6. ☐ ____ ____

7. ☐ ____ ____

8. ☐ ____ ____

9. ☐ ____ ____

REARRANGE THE NOTES   2–18

Write the letter names under each of the following groups of notes. Then, rearrange the letters
to spell a word under the second set of staff lines. Also rearrange the notes to match their letter
names. The first one is done to show you how.

1. $\overline{\text{G}}$ B A _____   _____   _____   _____

2.   B   A $\overline{\text{G}}$ _____   _____   _____   _____

3. _____   _____   _____   _____

4. _____   _____   _____   _____

5. _____   _____   _____   _____

6. _____   _____   _____   _____

FIGURE THE DIRECTION

The numbers and directions for this crossword puzzle were left out by the typist. Can you complete the puzzle without them? First write the words under each set of notes. Then figure out which direction and where each word should go. The puzzle is started for you so continue from there.

TREBLE CROSSWORD SQUARES   2–20

Each of these sets of notes spells a word. Read the notes from left to right and write the letters in order under the staff. Then, match the words with the numbers of the puzzle reading across and down, and write the words in the puzzle.

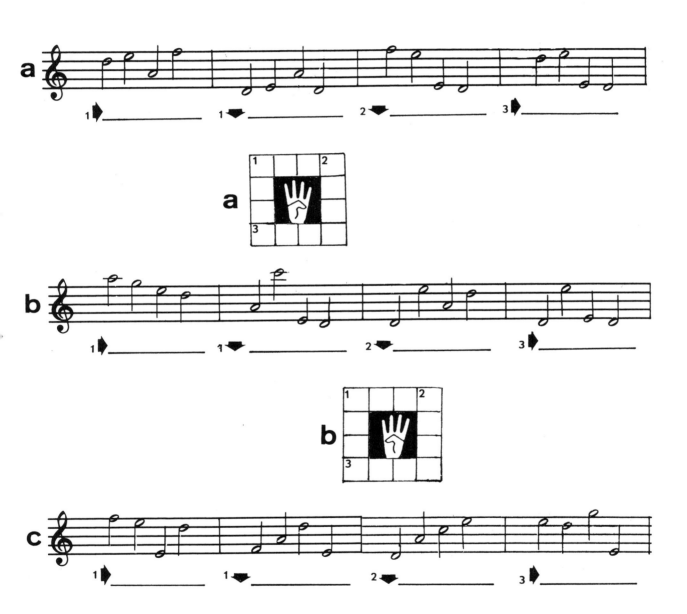

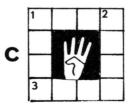

NICKNAMES   2–21

The letter names of the following groups of notes spell out popular nicknames. Write the nicknames under the staffs. Then, in the same order, write the long versions of the names on the chart.

1. _____

2. _____

3. _____

4. _____

5. _____

6. _____

a. _____

b. _____

c. _____

d. _____

e. _____

f. _____

MAKE A MUSICAL FAMILY TREE   2-22

Pretend that a friend has asked you to research his or her family tree. While at it, you discover that the first names of the people involved contain only the letters of the music alphabet—A B C D E F and G. As a result, you decide to surprise your friend by making a unique family tree, showing only the first names, all written in notes.

Draw whole notes on the staff to match the arrangement of letters in the names. The number "1" names go on the number "1" staff, and so on. These are the names:

    1. Ace, Bea   2. Abe, Edda   3. Gabe, Fae   4. Cab, Dag
       5. Ed, Deb   6. Ab, Ada   7. Eb, Bebe

After you have finished placing the notes on the staff, draw the faces of the family members.

TRANSPOSING

2–23

The transcriber of this tune copied it for a high soprano voice. Recopy it an octave lower, making it more suitable for group singing. After transposing it, write the letter names under the notes. Then figure out the title and write it on the blank. The first measure is done to show you how.

TITLE _____

BUILD IT OVER

2–24

Transpose this tune an octave lower using the treble staff. The bar lines are drawn for you. Draw the leger lines as carefully as possible. If you rewrite the song correctly, you will use 17 leger lines. The first note is done for you.

LONDON BRIDGE

Activities for
USING THE BASS (F) CLEF

Name _____   Score _____

Date _____   Class _____

LET'S PLAY BALL   2-25

Join the team if you can score 100%. These baseball terms all have one or more letters missing. Write the letters on the blanks, using letters from the music alphabet. Then, draw a matching whole note on the staff above each of your letters.

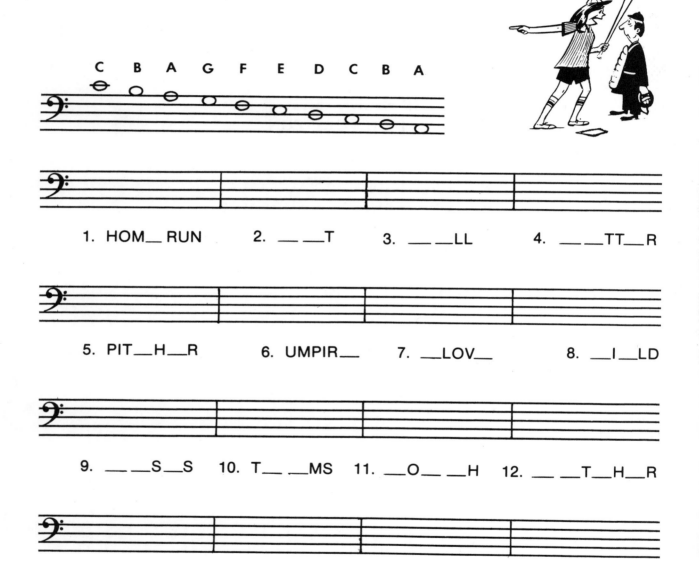

1. HOM__ RUN   2. __ __T   3. __ __LL   4. __ __TT__R

5. PIT__H__R   6. UMPIR__   7. __LOV__   8. __I __LD

9. __ __S__S   10. T__ __MS   11. __O__ __H   12. __ __T__H__R

13. INNIN__   14. STRIK__   15. M__SK   16. L__ __ __U__

NOTE THE NICKNAMES   2-26

The names on the scroll are the long versions of popular nicknames. Print the nickname under the staff using letters from the music alphabet. Then, draw the matching whole notes on the staff directly above the printed letters.

1. _____

2. _____

3. _____

4. _____

5. _____

Beatrice

Abel

Edgar

Adelaide

Edith

BASS CLEF PICTURE FUN

2–27

The names of these pictures can be spelled with notes. First print the name on the blank, using letters from the music alphabet. Allow spacing between the letters. Then, from left to right, draw whole notes on the staff above their letter names.

1. _____

2. _____

3. _____

4. _____

5. _____

6. _____

F CLEF PICTURE CLUE #1   2–28

Write the word under the staff that is suggested by the clue. All the letters are from the music alphabet, except the first letter, which you place in the box. Then, draw matching whole notes on the staff above the letters in the blanks. The picture gives the clue for the word that will be spelled out in the boxes.

1. A leaf from a book.
2. A notion; thought.
3. The green part that grows on a stem.
4. The opposite of "on."
5. A children's game.

1. □ ___ ___ ___

2. □ ___ ___ ___

3. □ ___ ___ ___

4. □ ___ ___

5. □ ___ ___

F CLEF PICTURE CLUE #2   2-29

Write the word under the staff that is suggested by the clue. All the letters are from the music alphabet except the first letter, which you place in the box. Then, draw matching whole notes on the staff above the letters on the blanks. The picture gives the clue for the word that will be spelled out in the boxes.

1. Free from harm.
2. To take notice of (rhymes with need).
3. Grass resembling bamboo (rhymes with deed).
4. Salt is sodium chlor __ __ __.
5. A spice which comes from the outer covering of the nutmeg (rhymes with lace).
6. A person's step (rhymes with face).

1. ☐ __ __ __

2. ☐ __ __ __

3. ☐ __ __ __

4. ☐ __ __

5. ☐ __ __ __

6. ☐ __ __ __

F CLEF MUSICAL ANAGRAM #1 2–30

Write the letter names of the following notes. You will find that each group of notes spells a word. Then, write the words on the grid, arranging them in such a way that the first vertical column reveals something about the picture.

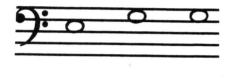

a. _____

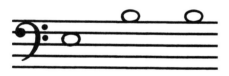

b. _____

c. _____

d. _____

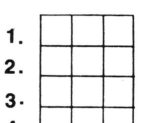

1.
2.
3.
4.

F CLEF MUSICAL ANAGRAM #2   2-31

Write the letter names of the following notes. You will find that each group of notes spells a word. Then, write the words on the grid, arranging them in such a way that the first vertical column reveals something about the picture.

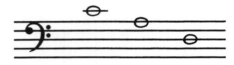

a. _____

b. _____

c. _____

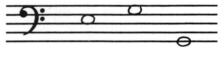

d. _____

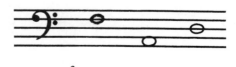

e. _____

f. _____

Clue: The word reading down rhymes with "erase."

F CLEF MUSICAL ANAGRAM #3   2–32

Write the letter names of the following notes. You will find that each group of notes spells a word. Then, write the words on the grid, arranging them in such a way that the first vertical column reveals something about the picture.

a. _____

b. _____

c. _____

d. _____

e. _____

f. _____

g. _____

	1.			
	2.			
	3.			
	4.			
	5.			
	6.			
	7.			

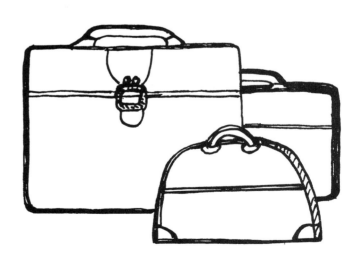

F CLEF MUSICAL ANAGRAM #4   2–33

Write the letter names of the following notes. You will find that each group of notes spells a
word. Then, write the words on the grid, arranging them in such a way that the first vertical
column reveals something about the picture.

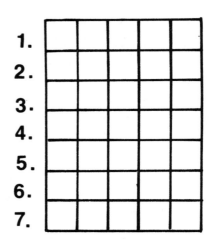

a. _____

b. _____

c. _____

d. _____

e. _____

f. _____

g. _____

1.
2.
3.
4.
5.
6.
7.

BASS CROSSWORD SQUARES

2–34

Each of these sets of notes spells a word. Read the notes from left to right and write the letters in order under the staff. Match the words with the numbers on the puzzle reading across and down. Then, rewrite the words in the puzzle.

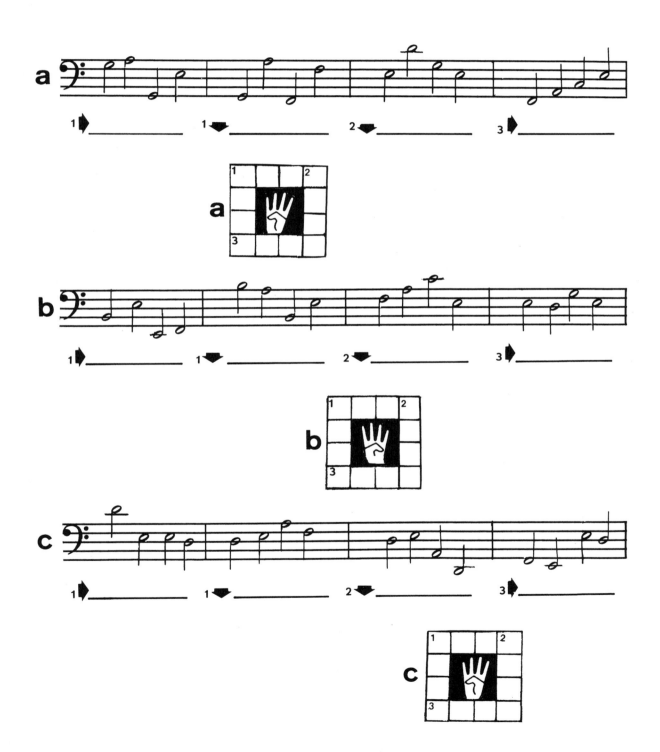

HIDDEN TREASURE

Look for the hidden treasure at the bottom of the sea to find the missing last letters for each of these words spelled out in notes. First, write the letters directly under the notes. Then, use a letter from the bottom of the sea to finish each word. Use each letter only once.

1. __ __ __ __

2. __ __ __

3. __ __ __

4. __ __ __ __

5. __ __ __ __

6. __ __ __

7. __ __ __ __

8. __ __ __ __

Activities for
USING BOTH TREBLE AND BASS CLEFS

IT'S ROUNDUP TIME   2-36

Find all of the space notes and circle them on the staffs. Then, write the letter names under them. Each set of circled notes in order will spell a word. Check your answers with the words in the lasso.

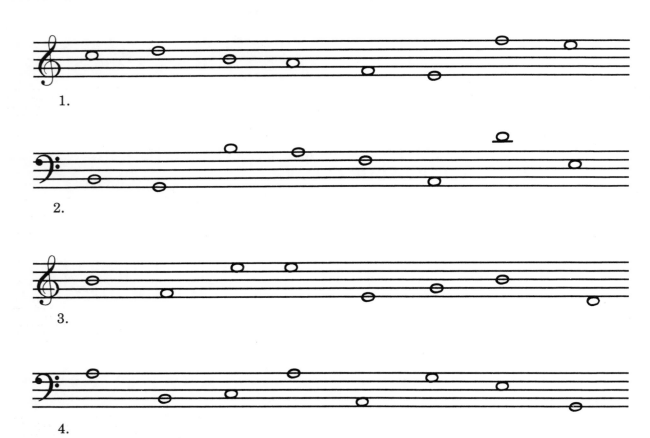

1.

2.

3.

4.

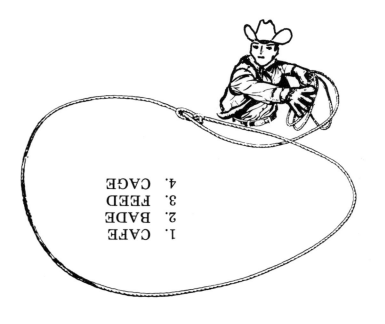

1. CAFE
2. BADE
3. FEED
4. CAGE

HERE'S THE PITCH

Find all the line notes and circle them on the staffs. Then, write the letter names under them. Each set of circled notes in order will spell a word. Check your answers with the words in the baseball at the bottom of the page.

1.

2.

3.

4.

1. BEAD
2. FACE
3. GAGE
4. DEAF

REWRITE AN OLD-FASHIONED TUNE

Rewrite this song using the treble clef, making it an octave higher than the notes in the bass clef. The first note is done for you.

After you have finished, circle all of the flatted notes.

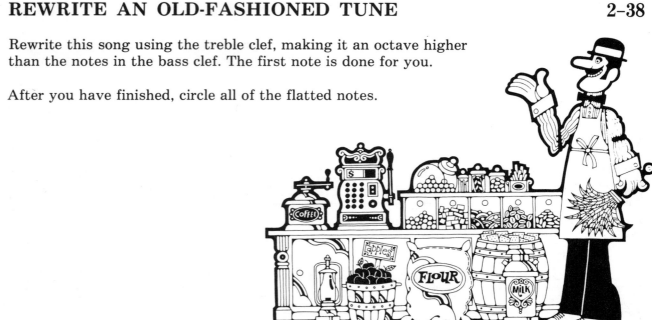

OATS, PEAS, BEANS AND BARLEY GROW

Name _____

Date _____

Score _____

Class _____

CHART YOUR COURSE

2–39

Rewrite this tune an octave lower, using the bass clef. The first note is done for you.

THE SPELLING TRIADS

Write the letter names of the triads in the boxes below the staff. For each group of triads, the circled squares from left to right will spell a word.

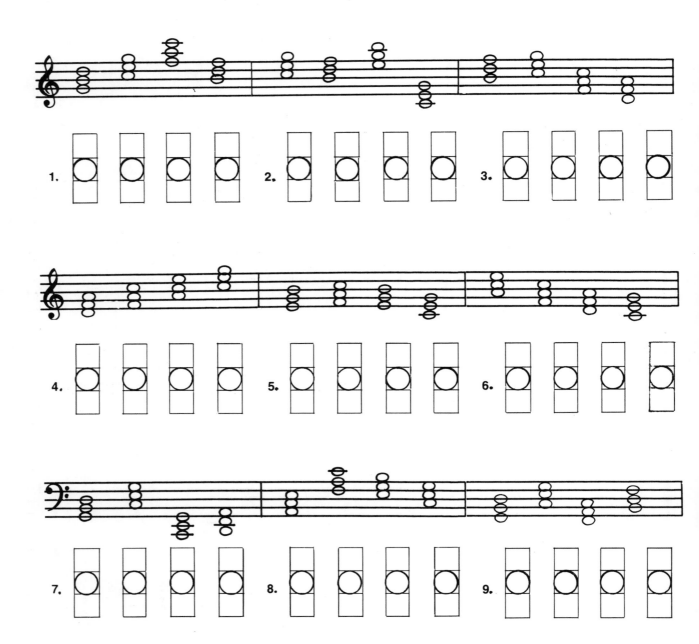

TRANSCRIBING IN OCTAVES

Place the proper clef sign on each staff of this song and draw the notes above their letter names. Use the note key to decide what type of notes to use. After you have finished, figure out the title and write it on the blank.

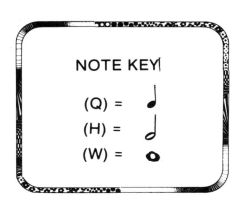

NOTE KEY
(Q) = ♩
(H) = ♪
(W) = ○

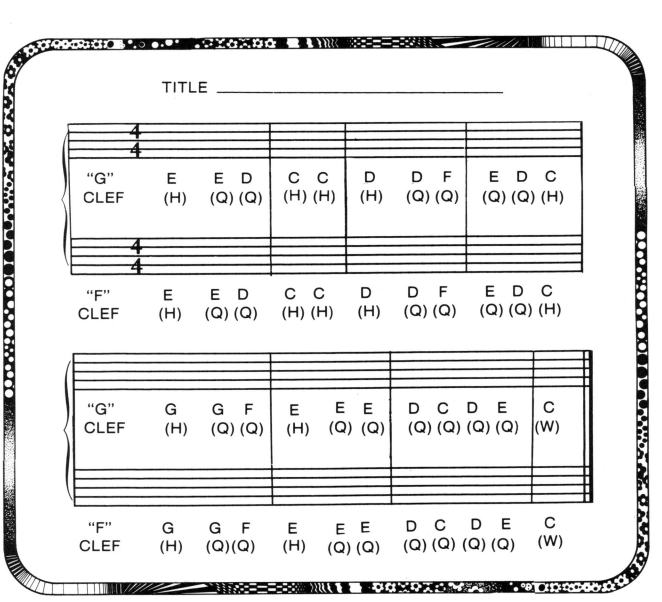

NAME THE KIDS

2–42

Write the letter names of the following groups of notes. Then, under the second set of staff lines, rearrange the letters to spell the names of eight kids. Draw the notes to match the new arrangement of letters. The girls' names will appear with the treble clef and the boys' names with the bass clef.

1. _____   _____

2. _____   _____

3. _____   _____

4. _____   _____

5. _____   _____

6. _____   _____

7. _____   _____

8. _____   _____

Activities for
USING THE G CLEF OR THE CLEF OF
ONE'S OWN INSTRUMENT

SHORT STUFF   2–43

This list of words can all be abbreviated with letters from the music alphabet. Write the abbreviation by the matching number below the staff. Then, use whole notes and draw them directly above their letter names.

1. Bachelor of Arts	8. District of Columbia
2. Account	9. Each
3. Advertisement	10. Federal Communications Commission
4. Before Christ	11. District Attorney
5. For example	12. Georgia
6. February	
7. Edition	

1. _____   2. _____   3. _____   4. _____

5. _____   6. _____   7. _____   8. _____

9. _____   10. _____   11. _____   12. _____

PICTURE DICTIONARY PAGE   2-44

The names of these pictures have two or more letters missing. Finish writing the names, using letters from the music alphabet. Then, draw a G clef or the clef of the instrument you play and carefully place a matching whole note ($\circ$) on the staff directly above each of your letters.

1. __ PPL __   2. __ UTT __ R __ LY   3. __ __ R

4. __ R __ SS   5. __ __ __   6. __ RO __

MATCH NOTES ON THE KEYBOARD   2–45

Draw the notes on the staff to match the dotted keys on the keyboard. Then, name the notes under the staff.

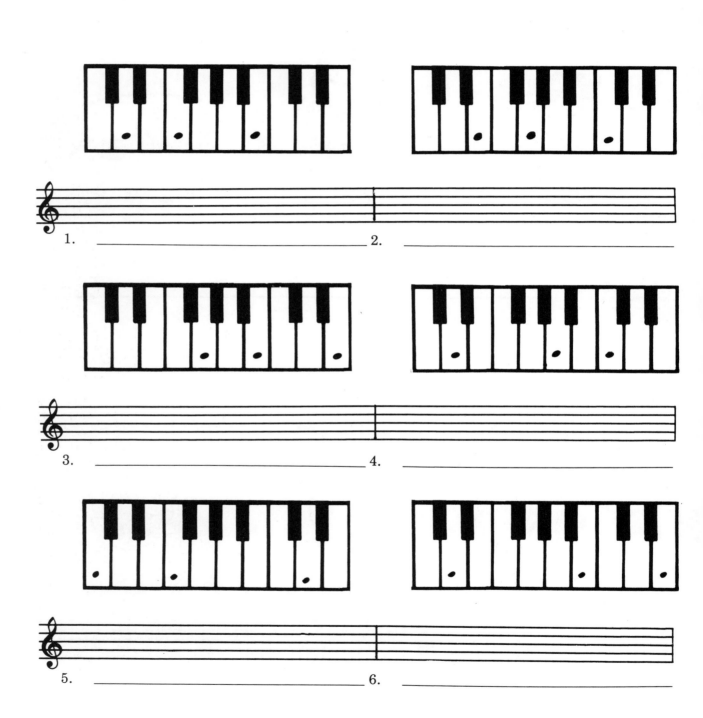

1. _____   2. _____

3. _____   4. _____

5. _____   6. _____

WHAT'S THE CLUE?   2–46

Here are the answers to a crossword puzzle. Your job is to write the clues. First, draw a G clef or the clef of the instrument you play on the staff. Then, draw whole notes, matching them with their letter names on the puzzle.

ACROSS

1 ⇨

2 ⇨

3 ⇨

4 ⇨

5 ⇨

DOWN

2 ⇩

Crossword grid:

	¹b	e	⁶d
⁷b			e
a			e
²a	d	d	e	d
g
³e	d	g	⁸e
⁴f	a	c	e	d	g
e					g
e					e
			⁵f	e	d

4 ⇩   6 ⇩   7 ⇩   8 ⇩

A MUSICAL SPELL-DOWN #1

The names of these pictures have three or more letters missing. Finish writing the names, using letters from the music alphabet. Then, draw a G clef or the clef of the instrument you play at the beginning of each staff. Carefully place a matching quarter note on the staff directly above each of your letters. Position all the notes on the staff for the stems to go downward (♩).

1. S _ N _ WI _ H   2. _ H _ RRI _ S   3. Z _ _ R _

4. _ _ _ TH _ R   5. J _ _ K _ T   6. V _ L _ NTIN _

Name _____   Score _____

Date _____   Class _____

A MUSICAL SPELL-DOWN #2   2–48

The names of these pictures have two or more letters missing. Finish writing the names, using letters from the music alphabet. Then, draw a G clef or the clef of the instrument you play and carefully place a matching eighth note on the staff directly above each of your letters. Position all the notes on the staff for the stems to go downward (♪).

1. _ R _ _ _ _   2. _ _ T _   3. _ _ K _

4. _ UTT _ R _ LY   5. _ _ L _ RY   6. _ _ _ _ R

Name _____   Score _____

Date _____   Class _____

PLAY WHAT YOU WRITE   2–49

Draw a G clef or the clef of the instrument you play at the beginning of both staffs. Then, use the letter names and types of notes indicated below to draw the notes on the staff. After you finish transcribing the song, play it on your instrument.

NOTE KEY

Q = ♩

H = ♪

"ODE TO JOY"

Ludwig van Beethoven

| (NOTE NAMES) | E | E | F | G | G | F | E | D | C | C | D | E | | E | D | D |
| (TYPES) | Q | Q | Q | Q | Q | Q | Q | Q | Q | Q | Q | Q | | Q | Q | H |

| | E | E | F | G | G | F | E | D | C | C | D | E | | D | C | C |
| | Q | Q | Q | Q | Q | Q | Q | Q | Q | Q | Q | Q | | Q | Q | H |

Name _____   Score _____

Date _____   Class _____

NAME THE SYMBOLS   2–50

The names of these music symbols have one or more letters missing. Finish writing the names using letters from the music alphabet. Then, draw a G clef or the clef of the instrument you play at the beginning of each staff. Place an eighth note directly above each of your letters. Watch the stem and flag direction (♪ ♭).

   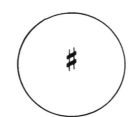   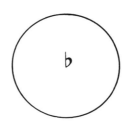

1. TR __ __ L__ __L __ __   2. SH __ RP   3. __ L __ T

   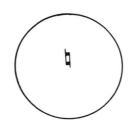   

4. __ __ SS __L __ __   5. N __ TUR __ L   6. ST __ __ __ __

Answer Key for
Reading and Writing Music

For students who are just beginning note reading, "Study Guide Strips" have been created as an aid. (Those particular activity sheets suitable for the Guide are indicated with an asterisk after the activity title.) The page is designed to be duplicated and cut into strips. Place these strips in an accessible area to have on hand and ready to use. Prior to distributing any note reading activity, discuss the range of notes to be used for answers.

2–1 IT'S YOUR GUESS

Answers for the intended words will vary. Suggestions are given here in parentheses.

1. dag (dog)
2. cad (cat)
3. gaga (grandpa)
4. baba (bottle)

5. dada (daddy)
6. bebe (baby)
7. fee (feed)
8. gede (kitty, spaghetti)

2–2 ALIEN TALK

1. face
2. feed
3. egg
4. cabbage

5. beef
6. cafe
7. deaf
8. bed

2–3 CAN YOU PICTURE THAT?

Answers are given in order of appearance in story:

age, Ada, dad, Bebe, bad, Ada, bed, egg, cab, Ada, face, Bebe, bad, Bad, Bebe, cage, bed, Bebe

2–4 MUSICAL G CLEF ANAGRAM #1

1. cab (c)
2. age (a)
3. gee (b)
4. egg (d)

2–5 MUSICAL G CLEF ANAGRAM #2

1. fade (d)
2. abed (c)
3. cafe (b)
4. edge (a)

2–6 MUSICAL G CLEF ANAGRAM #3

When two words begin with the same letter, place them in alphabetical order on the grid.

1. face (e)
2. abed (c)
3. cede (d)

4. aged (b)
5. deaf (f)
6. edge (a)

56

2-7 NEW-AGE NAMES

1. Ada
2. Decca
3. Deedee
4. Aca
5. Dacee
6. Ega

7. Agda
8. Fabe
9. Edda
10. Abbe
11. Gadee
12. Afee

2-8 MAKE A LIST

Answers will vary.

2-9 TREBLE CLEF PICTURE FUN*

1. CAB
2. ACE
3. BAG

4. FACE
5. BEE
6. BED

2-10 NAME THE PERCUSSION*

1. BASS DRUM
2. TRIANGLE
3. CYMBALS

4. CHIMES
5. TAMBOURINE
6. SNARE DRUM

2-11 THE EEEEEASY CIRCLES

A.

1. DFĒE
2. DĒĒG
3. EDDĒ
4. BĒFĒ

B.

1. GAEG
2. ĒFAC̄
3. ACGE
4. ADĒF

It may be necessary to provide an additional clue for 2A: GEE (verb) "command to horses to turn to the right." Use past tense.

2-12 WRITE THE ENDING

The two words formed in the story are ABE and CABBAGE. The rest of the answers will vary.

2-13 ADD A LETTER

1. D or F
   DACE or FACE
2. D or F
   DEED or FEED
3. B or F
   BADE or FADE

4. C or G
   CAGE or GAGE
5. C
   CAFE
6. D
   DEAF

2-14 TREASURE HUNT

Select from these answers, but use each letter only once:

1. hedge, ledge, sedge, wedge
2. beef, reef
3. lab, nab, tab
4. bade, wade

5. lace, race
6. heed, need, reed, seed, teed, weed
7. bad, had, lad, sad, tad, wad
8. rage, sage, wage

2-15   **G CLEF PICTURE CLUE #1***

1. FEW
2. AGO
3. DEER
4. BACK

2-16   **G CLEF PICTURE CLUE #2***

1. SAFE
2. WEED
3. ICED
4. MADE

2-17   **G CLEF PICTURE CLUE #3***

1. PAD
2. ODE
3. LEG
4. LAD
5. UBE
6. TAB
7. ICE
8. ODD
9. NAB

2-18   **REARRANGE THE NOTES***

	A.	B.	C.	D.
1.	GBA	GEG	DDA	EDB
2.	BAG	EGG	DAD or ADD	BED or DEB
3.	GADE	CEAF	BEDA	GEED
4.	AGED	CAFE or FACE	BEAD	EDGE
5.	EDFE	GAEG	FCAE	EGB
6.	FEED	GAGE	FACE or CAFE	BEG

2-19   **FIGURE THE DIRECTION**

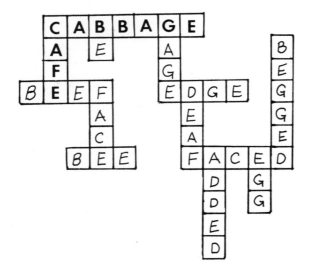

2-20 TREBLE CROSSWORD SQUARES

a. DEAF, DEAD, FEED, DEED

b. AGED, ACED, DEAD, DEED

c. FEED, FADE, DACE, EDGE

2-21 NICKNAMES

1. Ed—Edwin, Edward, Edgar, Edwina
2. Deb—Deborah
3. Abe—Abraham, Abel
4. Fae—Fayette, Faith
5. Bab—Barbara
6. Deedee—Diedre, Diane

2-22 MAKE A MUSICAL FAMILY TREE*

Placement of notes on the staff will vary.

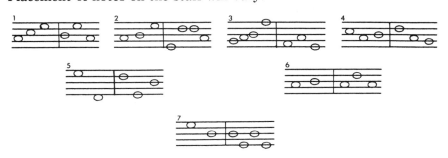

2-23 TRANSPOSING*

Title of song is "Yankee Doodle."
FF / GA / FA / G— / FF / GA / F— / E—
FF / GA / BA / GF / EC / DE / F   / F

2-24 BUILD IT OVER*

DEDC / BCD— / ABC— / BCD— / DEDC / BCD— / A—D— / BG ◼

2-25 **LET'S PLAY BALL**

1. HOMERUN
2. BAT
3. BALL
4. BATTER
5. PITCHER
6. UMPIRE
7. GLOVE
8. FIELD
9. BASES
10. TEAMS
11. COACH
12. CATCHER
13. INNING
14. STRIKE
15. MASK
16. LEAGUE

2-26 **NOTE THE NICKNAMES***

1. Bea
2. Abe
3. Ed
4. Ad or Adde
5. Ede or Dee

2-27 **BASS CLEF PICTURE FUN***

1. CAB
2. ACE
3. BAG
4. FACE
5. BEE
6. BED

2-28 **F CLEF PICTURE CLUE #1***

1. PAGE
2. IDEA
3. LEAF
4. OFF
5. TAG

2-29 **F CLEF PICTURE CLUE #2***

1. SAFE
2. HEED
3. REED
4. IDE
5. MACE
6. PACE

2-30 **F CLEF MUSICAL ANAGRAM #1**

1. BED (d)
2. EBB (c)
3. EGG (a)
4. FED (b)

2-31 **F CLEF MUSICAL ANAGRAM #2**

1. DAD (d)
2. EBB (e)
3. FAD (f)
4. AGE (a)
5. CAD (b)
6. EGG (c)

2–32   F CLEF MUSICAL ANAGRAM #3

1. BEAD (c)
2. ABED (d)
3. GAFF (g)
4. GAGE (b)
5. AGED (f)
6. GEED (e)
7. EDGE (a)

2–33   F CLEF MUSICAL ANAGRAM #4

1. CADGE (b)
2. ABACA (d)
3. BAAED (e)
4. BADGE (f)
5. ADAGE (a)
6. GAGED (g)
7. EDGED (c)

2–34   BASS CROSSWORD SQUARES

a.   GAGE   GAFF   EDGE   FACE

b.   BEEF   BABE   FACE   EDGE

c.   DEED   DEAF   DEAD   FEED

2–35   HIDDEN TREASURE

1. FACES
2. DECK
3. DECAL
4. BADGER
5. ABBEY
6. DEADEN
7. BEACH
8. AFFECT

2–36 IT'S ROUNDUP TIME

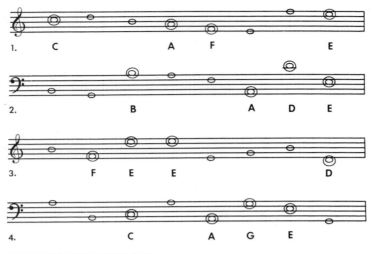

1.   C   A   F   E

2.   B   A   D   E

3.   F   E   E   D

4.   C   A   G   E

2–37 HERE'S THE PITCH

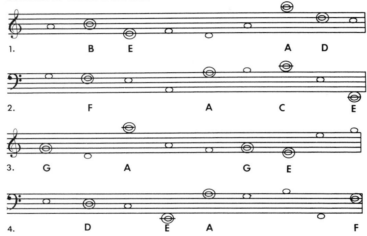

1.   B   E   A   D

2.   F   A   C   E

3.   G   A   G   E

4.   D   E   A   F

2–38 REWRITE AN OLD-FASHIONED TUNE*

AAAG / FFF / B♭B♭B♭A / GGGG
AB♭CB♭ / AAB♭CA / GB♭AG / FFF

2–39 CHART YOUR COURSE*

BAGA / BBB / AAA / BDD / BAGA / BBB / AABA / G

2–40 THE SPELLING TRIADS

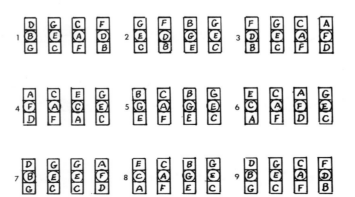

2-41 TRANSCRIBING IN OCTAVES*

Title of the song is "Go Tell Aunt Rhodie." Answers can be checked with the Study Guide Strips.

2-42 NAME THE KIDS

1. EAF — FAE	2. BED — DEB
2. BEA — ABE	6. BBEA — BABE (Babe Ruth)
3. BBA — BAB	7. DDEE — DEDE
4. GEBA — GABE	8. DE — ED

2-43 SHORT STUFF*

1. BA	4. BC	7. ed	10. FCC
2. Ac or Acc	5. eg	8. DC	11. DA
3. ad	6. Feb	9. ea	12. GA

2-44 PICTURE DICTIONARY PAGE*

1. **APPLE**	4. **DRESS**
2. **BUTTERFLY**	5. **EGG**
3. **CAR**	6. **FROG**

2-45 MATCH NOTES ON THE KEYBOARD*

1. DFB	4. DAC
2. EGC	4. CFD
3. GBE	6. DBE

2-46 WHAT'S THE CLUE?*

Answers can be checked with the Study Guide Strips.

2-47 A MUSICAL SPELL-DOWN #1*

1. SANDWICH	4. FEATHER
2. CHERRIES	5. JACKET
3. ZEBRA	6. VALENTINE

2-48 A MUSICAL SPELL-DOWN #2*

1. BREAD	4. BUTTERFLY
2. GATE	5. CELERY
3. CAKE	6. BEAR

2-49 PLAY WHAT YOU WRITE*

Answers can be checked with the Study Guide Strips.

2-50 NAME THE SYMBOLS*

1. TREBLE CLEF	4. BASS CLEF
2. SHARP	5. NATURAL
3. FLAT	6. STAFF

Clefs for Commonly Used Instruments and Voices

➤ 𝄞	This is the G clef. This clef points to G located on the second line. Notice how the curved line of the clef draws a ring around the second line. A staff with this clef is called the Treble Staff. The treble staff is most commonly used for general classroom music instruction. Children's singing voices and typical classroom instruments use this clef.

Clef Name	These instruments use the treble clef:			
	Strings	*Percussion*	*Wind*	*Voices*
Treble Clef or G Clef	Guitar Ukulele Banjo Violin Harp	Piano (right hand) Xylophone Chimes Glockenspiel Vibraphone Marimba	Cornet Trumpet Flugelhorn French horn Tenor Trombone Euphonium Piccolo Flute Oboe Clarinet Alto Clarinet Bass Clarinet Bassoon English Horn Saxophone	Children's Singing voices Soprano (Female) Alto (Female) Tenor (Male)

➤ 𝄢	This is the F clef. The "head" of the clef rests on the fourth line, which is F. The other notes run in order up and down the staff, with G in the space above F, and so on. A staff with this clef is called the Bass Staff. The bass staff is used for some men's singing voices and various instruments, including the left hand for keyboard instruments.

Clef Name	These instruments use the bass clef.			
	Strings	*Percussion*	*Wind*	*Voices*
Bass Clef or F Clef	Cello Bass Harp	Piano (left hand) Timpani Marimba	Bassoon Contrabassoon French Horn Trombone Tuba	Bass (Male)

Study Guide Strips

Photocopy as many pages as needed. Then cut apart along the dotted lines. Store in easy accessible 3″ × 5″ file box.

Use these "Study Guide Strips" as:

- an aid in completing activities

- as a device for self-checking

- as a pocket study guide for reviewing and studying notes

Note placement on the Treble of "G" Staff

C D E F G A B C D E F G A B C

Note placement on the Bass or "F" Staff

C B A G F E D C B A G F E D C

Note placement on the Grand Staff with keyboard

C D E F G A B middle C D E F G A B C

Progress Chart for
Reading and Writing Music

Use this chart to keep a record of activities completed for each class. List your classes (or students) in the given spaces at the right. As each activity is completed for a class, mark an "X" in the appropriate column.

Activity Number/Title		Skill Involved				
Using the Treble (G) Clef						
2-1	IT'S YOUR GUESS	Naming notes from low "C" to high "E"				
2-2	ALIEN TALK	Naming notes from low "C" to high "E"				
2-3	CAN YOU PICTURE THAT?	Using letter names of notes to write words				
2-4	MUSICAL G CLEF ANAGRAM #1	Writing words on a grid from notes to figure out puzzle theme				
2-5	MUSICAL G CLEF ANAGRAM #2	Writing words on a grid from notes to figure out puzzle theme				
2-6	MUSICAL G CLEF ANAGRAM #3	Writing words on a grid from notes to figure out puzzle theme				
2-7	NEW-AGE NAMES	Writing new names of the future using letter names of notes				
2-8	MAKE A LIST	Creating a list of words from the Music Alphabet				
2-9	TREBLE CLEF PICTURE FUN	Writing names of objects using notes and note names				
2-10	NAME THE PERCUSSION	Writing names of percussion instruments using notes and note names				
2-11	THE EEEEEASY CIRCLES	Unscrambling sets of notes to spell words				
2-12	WRITE THE ENDING	Writing a story using notes for words				
2-13	ADD A LETTER	Adding the first note to spell words on the staff				
2-14	TREASURE HUNT	Writing words from notation using given first letters				

Activity Number/Title		Skill Involved				

Using the G Clef or the Clef of One's Own Instrument

	Activity	Skill Involved				
2-43	SHORT STUFF	Writing abbreviations with letters and notes from the Music Alphabet				
2-44	PICTURE DICTIONARY PAGE	Notating and writing missing letters in words to match pictures				
2-45	MATCH NOTES ON THE KEYBOARD	Drawing and naming notes from keyboard clues				
2-46	WHAT'S THE CLUE?	Writing questions for a crossword puzzle in notation				
2-47	A MUSICAL SPELL-DOWN #1	Writing missing letters of words to match pictures and notating on a staff				
2-48	A MUSICAL SPELL-DOWN #2	Writing missing letters of words to match pictures and notating on a staff				
2-49	PLAY WHAT YOU WRITE	Transcribing "Ode to Joy"				
2-50	NAME THE SYMBOLS	Writing notes and filling in letters to name symbols				

Reading and Writing Music

word list

bass clef
bass staff
chords
clef
eighth note
"F" clef
flag
flat
"G" clef
half note
high "C"
keyboard
leger line
letter names
line note
lines

measure
middle "C"
music alphabet
octave
quarter note
rest
sharp
space note
spaces
staff
stem
transcribe
transpose
treble clef
treble staff

Craft Project for
Reading and Writing Music

MUSICAL MOBILE

Objective: The Musical Mobile is designed to provide a fun method of learning and to stimulate the student's increase in memorizing the symbols for notation and rests.

Materials Needed:

- Copies of the sheet of patterns
- Ruler (optional)
- Scissors
- Pen or felt-tipped markers
- Colored yarn or string
- Pointed object such as a pencil or compass

Construction Directions:

1. You might want to decorate or draw staff lines to follow the shape of the spiral.
2. Use scissors to cut around the circle and along the dotted lines of the spiral. Hold the spiral by the center and the end. Then, gently pull it open. Make a hole through each dot of the spiral. (See the illustration.)

3. Cut out the squares along the dotted lines. Carefully make a hole through each dot of the squares with a pencil or compass point. Darken the symbols with a pen or felt-tipped marker, and draw a matching symbol on the opposite side of each square.

4. Measure a short piece of yarn, enough to tie two knots and to extend eight or ten inches in length. When you have determined the right measurement, cut the other nine pieces of yarn the same length. Thread a piece of yarn through the hole in the square and tie a knot to attach the yarn. (It may be necessary to poke the yarn through the hole with a pencil or compass point.) Pull the other end of the yarn through the hole from the underside of the spiral. Allow the square to hang about eight or ten inches from the spiral. Tie a knot to secure the yarn to the spiral.

5. To suspend the spiral, make a knot at one end of a longer piece of yarn. Pull the other end through the hole in the center of the spiral from the underside. Make a hanging loop at the top of the yarn and suspend the mobile from the ceiling. (See the illustration.)

Uses: The following ideas are only suggestions for incorporating the musical mobile into classroom study to bring out meaningful relationships and concepts in a creative way.

1. After initially constructing the spiral, add each new symbol as it is learned. Use the envelope from the craft project of Unit 6 to store symbols.

2. Construct the spiral before the symbols are learned, and as the student becomes familiar with each new symbol, draw the symbol on the back of the matching square. When the clefs, notes, and rests are all learned, the backs of the squares will then be complete.

3. Allow the student to figure out a logical sequence of squares before attaching them to the spiral. The notes might be grouped together along with the rests, then the clefs; or the clefs might come first, then the notes and rests arranged according to their duration.

4. Use the mobile as an incentive for students to construct when these symbols are learned.

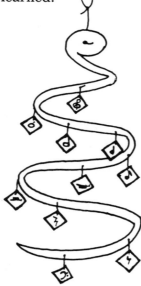

Name ______________________________

Date ______________________________

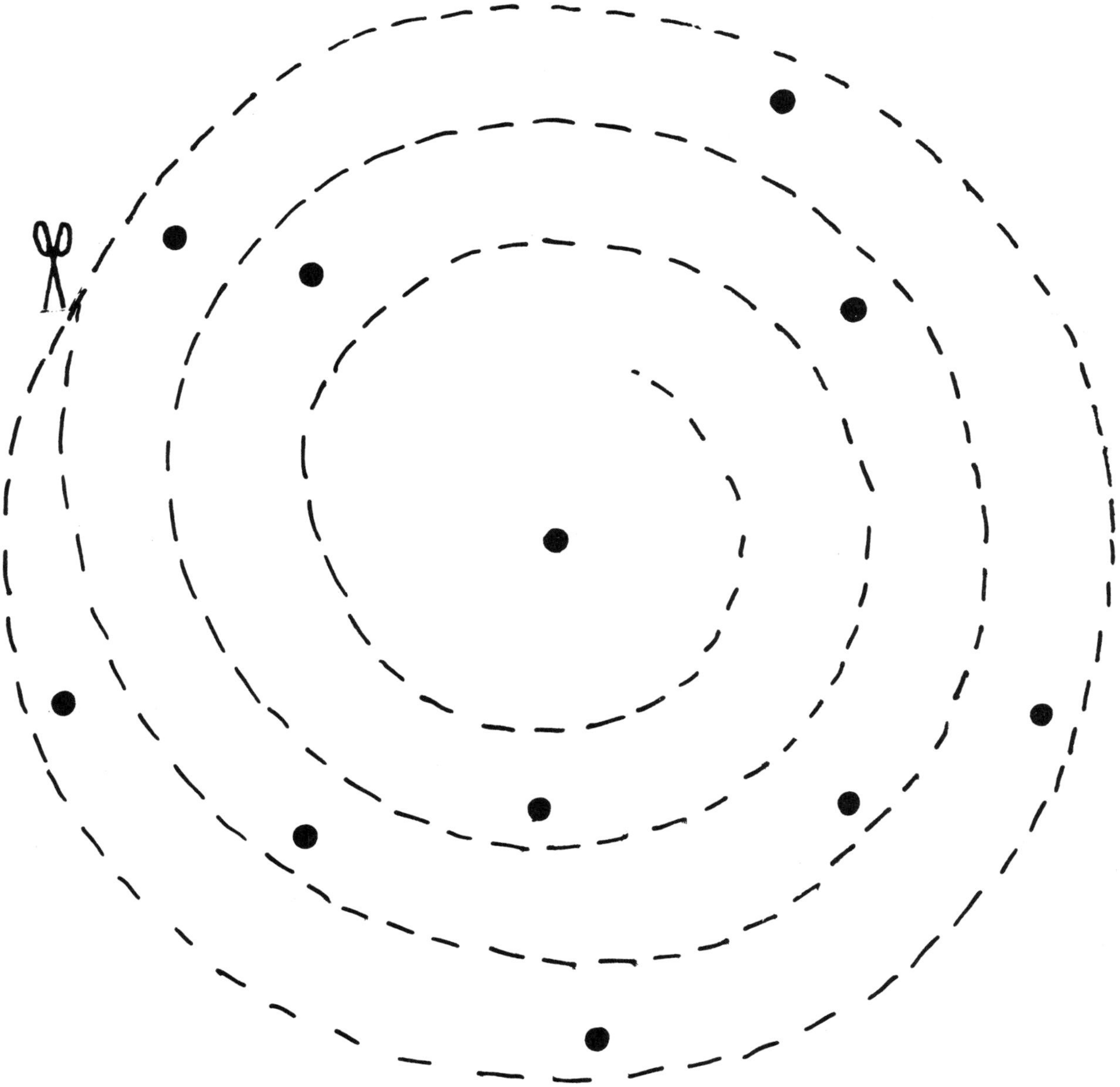

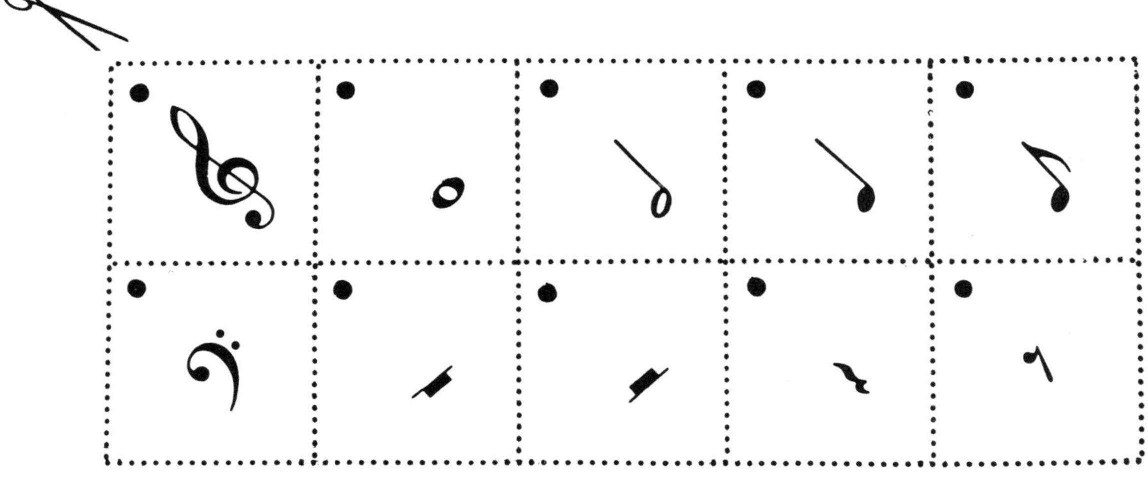

Incentive Badges

To the teacher: Cut apart badges and keep in a handy 3″ × 5″ file box along with tape. Encourage students to write their names and the date on the backs of their badges and to wear them.

MUSIC AWARD

A Pledge

DO IT NOW!

_____
_____
_____
(name)

MUSIC TOKEN

MUSIC AWARD

THANKS

BEST BEHAVIOR

"Busy as a bee"

MUSIC AWARD

CERTIFICATE

TO: FOR:

DOUBLE EXTRA BONUS

MUSIC AWARD

NAME _____

_____

WITH THIS COUPON . . .

NAME _____

IS ENTITLED TO _____

_____

_____

MUSIC AWARD

For hopping to it!
Good helper badge
in music class.

Watch
OUT!

Best in the class . . . .
MUSIC AWARD

Creative WRITING

MUSIC CLASS AWARD

Great News

best   work

MUSIC AWARD

DOG GONE GOOD
MUSIC AWARD!

(name)

WELCOME

to
MUSIC CLASS

Congratulations!

creative drawing
MUSIC AWARD

1st

Best performer
in
Music Class!

DON'T FORGET!

MUSIC

MUSIC SHARE-A-GRAM

TO: _____ DATE _____
(Parent's Name)

FROM: _____ SCHOOL _____
(Classroom Music Teacher)

RE: _____ CLASS _____
(Student's Name)

To help you recognize your child's success in music class or any area that needs attention the following observation(s) has/have been made.

	Exceptional	Satisfactory	Unsatisfactory
Shows musical aptitude			
Shows creativity			
Shows talent			
Shows initiative			
Self-concept in music class			
Fairness in dealing with classmates			
Self-direction			
Care of instrument and equipment			
Reaction to constructive criticism			
Observes music class rules			
Starts and completes work on time			
Generally follows directions			

over for comments ▶

- -

RETURN-A-GRAM

TO: _____ DATE _____
(Classroom Music Teacher)

FROM: _____ SCHOOL _____
(Parent's Name)

RE: _____ CLASS _____
(Student's Name)

Please write your comments or questions on the back and return. If you want to be called for a parent-teacher conference, indicate below.

STUDENT RECORD PROFILE CHART

_____ (Student's Name)   Class _____   Year _____

Select the appropriate data in parentheses for each category, i, ii, iii, and iv, and record the information in the chart below as shown in the example.

i.—Unit Number for *Music Curriculum Activities Library* (1, 2, 3, 4, 5, 6, 7)

ii.—Date (Day/Month)

iii.—Semester (1, 2, 3, 4) or Summer School: Session 1 (S1), Session 2 (S2)

iv.—Score: Select one of the three grading systems, a., b., or c., that applies to your school progress report and/or applies to the specific activity.

a.

(O)	= Outstanding
(G)	= Good
(S)	= Satisfactory
(NI)	= Needs Improvement
(U)	= Unsatisfactory
(I)	= Incomplete
(—)	= Absent

b.

(A)	= 93–100 [percentage score]
(B)	= 85–92
(C)	= 75–84
(D)	= 70–74
(F)	= 0–69
(I)	= Incomplete
(—)	= Absent

c.

(R/P):	
R	= Correct number of responses.
P	= Possible correct number of responses.
(I)	= Incomplete
(—)	= Absent

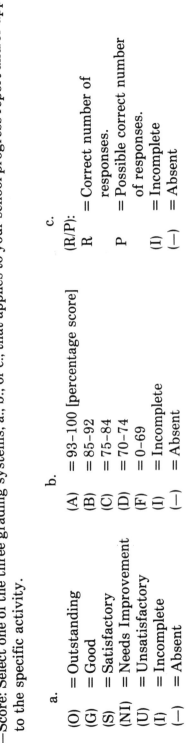

i	ii
iii	iv

_____ Class _____ Year _____

Student's Name

MUSIC SELF-IMPROVEMENT CHART (for student use)

a. On the back of this chart write your goal(s) for music class at the beginning of each semester.
b. On a separate sheet record the date and each new music skill you have acquired during the semester.
c. MUSIC SHARE-A-GRAM (date sent to parent)

d. RETURN-A-GRAM (date returned to teacher)

e. MUSIC AWARD BADGES (date and type rec'd)

1.
2.
3.

f. SPECIAL MUSIC RECOGNITION (date and type rec'd)

1.
2.
3.

g. SPECIAL MUSIC EVENT ATTENDANCE RECORD (date and name of special performance, recital, rehearsal, concert, field trip, film, workshop, seminar, institute, etc.)

1.
2.
3.
4.

h. ABOVE AND BEYOND: Extra Credit Projects (date and name of book report, classroom performance, construction of hand-made instrument, report on special music performance on TV, etc.)

1.
2.
3.
4.

i. PROGRESS REPORT/REPORT CARD RECORD (semester and grade received)

1.
2.
3.
4.

j. MUSIC SIGN-OUT RECORD (name of instrument, music, book or equipment with sign-out date and due date)

1.
2.
3.
4.
5.

6.
7.
8.
9.
10.